Mark Flashman.

THE WORZEL G
COOKBOOK

'I'm Worzel Gummidge and this 'ere's my cookbook.
'Seein' as 'ow I'm such a good cook, I thought I might share some o' my recipes with you.'

In this book Valerie Hall has written down recipes for some of the delicious food Worzel concocts when he has a chance to put on his 'cookin' 'ead'. And you don't have to be as messy as Worzel when you try out some of these scarecrow specials! They're easy and safe to make, require the minimum of cooking, and taste and look good when you've finished.

THE WORZEL GUMMIDGE COOKBOOK

Compiled by Valerie Hall
Illustrated by Lesley Smith
Diagrams by Chris Legee

KNIGHT BOOKS
Hodder and Stoughton

Copyright © Southern TV Ltd and
Walter Hall and Worzel Ltd
Illustrations copyright © Hodder and Stoughton Ltd, 1979
Diagrams Copyright © Hodder and Stoughton Ltd, 1979
First published by Knight Books 1979

*The characters and situations in this book are
entirely imaginary and bear no relation to any real
person or actual happening*

This book is sold subject to the condition that
it shall not, by way of trade or otherwise, be
lent, re-sold, hired out or otherwise circulated
without the publisher's prior consent in any
form of binding or cover other than that in
which this is published and without a similar
condition including this condition being
imposed on the subsequent purchaser.

Printed and bound in Great Britain for
Hodder and Stoughton Paperbacks, a
division of Hodder and Stoughton Ltd.,
Mill Road, Dunton Green, Sevenoaks,
Kent (Editorial Office: 47 Bedford
Square, London, WC1 3DP) by
C. Nicholls & Company Ltd.

ISBN 0 340 25243 X

CONTENTS

A MESSAGE FROM WORZEL GUMMIDGE

Good-day to 'ee

I'm Worzel Gummidge and this 'ere's my cookbook. I s'pose you knows as 'ow I've got lots of different 'eads – up in the old barn I keeps 'em. But I bet you didn't know that my favourite one's my cookin' 'ead. Only, trouble is, see, I don't get much charnst of trying out my famous scarecrow recipes – seein' as 'ow I don't 'ave no kitchen of my own, in a manner of speakin'.

Sometimes, though, my little robin tells me that the Braithwaites, as owns Scatterbrook Farm, 'ave gone away for the weekend. Or else that fat ol' baggage Mrs Bloomsbury-Barton's gone to town for the day to get 'erself beautifified – some 'opes!

Now then, them's the occashuns when I puts on my cookin' 'ead. An' I slips out o' Ten Acre Field and nips into one or t'other o' their kitchens. An' dang me, if I don't start straight in throwing ingredients about the place. They don't take kindly to the mess I've made when they comes back – but when you're as good a cook as me, you're bound to get a pound or two o' flour and a

1

couple o' dozen smashed eggs up the walls an' down the floor, so to speak.

Seein' as 'ow I'm such a good cook, I thought I might share some o' my recipes with you. Only thing is, I can't write. Not with having twigs for fingers. I do 'ave a writin' 'ead, o' course, same as I'm wearing now – on'y I 'as to take it off to put on my cookin' 'ead, d'y'see?

Anyways, these 'ere cookbook folk has sent down a dang dratted pesky woman so's I can tell to her my recipes. I hope she writes 'em down proper.

Fust off, I wants to tell you some things you gotter be very careful of when you're in a kitchen.

All us scarecrows is scared o' fire, as I s'pose you knows, 'cos it can do terrible things to one an' all – yumans as well as scarecrows. What I'm saying is, you gotter be very respeckful o' fire *and* any kind of heat. Don't go using no matches now, nor lighting any ovens neither. You better ask a grown-up to do that sort o' thing for you.

On top o' which, you oughter ask a grown-up to be in the kitchen with you while you're cookin' – if nothin' else, it'll keep all them bothersome growed-ups from gettin' underneath us scarecrows' feet!

Allus wear an apron too, that's another thing. An' wash your twigs an' straw . . . sorry, 'ands, afore you starts. *An'* wipe down the table-top.

Another thing, you gotter be *extra*-special careful when you uses a knife, 'cos if you cuts yoursel' see, the Crowman 'ee can't mend your fingers same as he mends our twigs.

Also, most important, you must read each recipe right through afore you starts, then you gets out the utensils you needs for it.

Don't forget to weigh or measure all the ingredients properly. 'Course, I don't never need to weigh nothin', I just slops it all in, but you ain't an expert same as me.

An' whenever you 'ave cause to go anywheres near anything that's hot, then you gotter wear them oven-glove contraptions.

This silly cookbook dang dratted woman says I've got to tell you to tidy up as you goes along, otherwise your mums won't let you use the kitchen again.

I reckons thass about all you need to know for starting off with – so now you can 'ave a go yourselves at makin' some o' the delishus things I makes when I gets my cookin' 'ead on. Course, when you've finished, all you'll be able to do is eat the dratted things. Not me – I slings most o' the things I make at Aunt Sally!

Worzel Gummidge

EDITOR'S NOTE

Worzel Gummidge has given you some sensible rules to follow to make sure you have fun **safely** in the kitchen.

One thing you should remember: always put on oven-gloves if you have to lift anything that's hot, otherwise as well as burning yourself, you'll probably drop whatever it is you're holding.

Recipes sometimes use words and terms you may not be familiar with. The following explanations should help you:

Beat, whip or **whisk** – to mix ingredients until they're well blended together, using an egg beater. Make sure you mix in all the bits from the side of the bowl so that none is wasted.

Blend together – to stir ingredients together in a bowl, usually with a wooden spoon, until they are very well mixed.

Cream – some recipes may ask you to cream butter or margarine and sugar together. To do this you soften the butter by mashing it against the side of the bowl with the back of a wooden spoon, mixing in the sugar. Then when it's softer, beat the mixture with the wooden spoon in a circular movement, until the butter and sugar look like thick cream.

Extract the juice – cut your fruit (oranges, lemons or grapefruit) in half. Holding one half firmly in your right hand (or left hand, if you're left-handed) push the fruit over the cup of the squeezer and twist it round and round until you've removed all the juice.

Grate – holding the grater steady with one hand, firmly push whatever it is you want to grate (cheese, carrots etc.) down the side with the size holes that you require, being very careful not to grate your fingers, until it's all pushed through. If the grater is not the kind that catches the grated cheese or carrot, remember to stand it on a plate or chopping boar.

Greased (or oiled) baking sheets – to prevent food like Easy Cheesy Puffs sticking to the tins they are baked on, take a small piece of butter or margarine (or a few drops of cooking oil) and smear it round the tin with a piece of greaseproof paper.

Heat-proof surface – a surface that is not harmed by having something hot put on it e.g. an asbestos mat or a wooden board, but not polished wood or a plastic tablecloth. If you're not sure where to find a heat-proof surface in your kitchen, ask a grown-up.

Knead – you may find you are asked to knead bits of pastry together. This is just another way of saying roll it into a ball.

Roll out pastry – pastry must be rolled lightly, and once you've put it down on a floured board you should not move it round or turn it over, just change the direction in which you're rolling to change the shape of the pastry. And remember to rub a little flour onto the rolling pin before you start.

Season – most things taste nicer with a little salt and pepper, and these are called seasonings. If a recipe tells you to season something, mix in a little of each, taste a tiny spoonful, and if it's not quite enough, add a little more. But don't add too much to start with – it's better to have too little seasoning than too much.

Shred – cut something very finely into thin strips, such as cabbage.

Sieve or **sift** – we do this to remove lumps or bits of things, such as lumps in flour or as in Raisin Popovers.

Strain – is to pour something through a sieve to get rid of bits and lumps; just the same as to sieve.

Do try and remember to have warmed plates ready for hot food, as this helps prevent food getting cold too quickly – and there's nothing worse than cold food that's meant to be hot. Some ovens have a grill beneath the rings which is a nice warm place to keep plates if the oven or one of the top rings is on. Otherwise, try putting the plates in a basin of warm water for five

6

minutes before you dish up, drying them thoroughly first of course.

If you follow these rules and the instructions given in each recipe, you'll find that cooking is great fun and much easier than you ever thought. As a guide, the more difficult recipes (ones which involve chopping vegetables, for instance) are marked with a star.

WORZEL'S KITCHEN CODE

So let's remember Worzel's Kitchen Code:

*Don't play with fire: ask a grown-up to light the oven for you, and always wear oven-gloves when lifting something hot.

*Wash your hands before you start.

*Wear an apron to keep your clothes clean.

*Read the recipe through before you start.

*Carefully weigh and measure all the ingredients you need.

*Get out all the tools (that's what grown-ups mean by utensils) you need before you start.

*Be very careful if you have to use sharp knives and scissors.

*Do remember to wash and clean up after you, so next you ask to use the kitchen the answer will be 'Yes, of course!'

*You will discover that though most of these recipes are for savoury foods, a few of the others – particularly those for puddings – use sugar. Brown sugar is better for everyone than white; and remember, too, after eating anything sweet, do clean your teeth! Humans, unlike scarecrows, get toothache unless they look after their teeth.

*And lastly, 'happy cooking'!

JACKET-TATERS

That Mr Shepherd might always be argufying with people, but 'e knows a good tater when 'e grows one. So when I fancies a nice 'ot jacket-tater, I nips down to 'is garden an' lifts a few of 'is King Edwards when 'is back's turned. Then I 'ops along to the Crowman's 'ouse an' shares them. Course, I daresn't tell 'im where they comes from – so don't you tell 'im neither.

Serves 4 people

Utensils needed: Baking sheet, kitchen paper, vegetable brush, knife, teaspoon, grater, oven-gloves.

Oven temperature: Gas mark 6, 400°F, 200°C. Before you start to scrub the potatoes, ask a grown-up to light the oven for you and to make sure there is a shelf near the top of the oven for you to use.

Cooking time: About 1½ hours.

A finished baked potato

Ingredients:
   4 medium-sized potatoes
   1 heaped teaspoon salt
   butter
   4 ounces (100g) cheddar cheese

Method:
   Scrub the potatoes with the vegetable brush in cold water until they are clean. Dry them on some kitchen paper. Take another sheet of kitchen paper and sprinkle the salt over it. Roll each potato in the salt, then place them on the baking

sheet. Put them in the oven and bake for about 1½ hours. While they are cooking, grate the cheese. To test if the potatoes are cooked, put on your oven-gloves, carefully take them out of the oven and squeeze one of them. If the inside 'gives' and feels soft, then it is cooked. When they are ready, cut a cross on the side uppermost and squeeze the potato – using oven-gloves, of course – so that the inside starts to pop out. Put a big knob of butter in the hole and about a tablespoon of cheese. When you have done this to all the potatoes, put them back into the oven for another 10 minutes or until the cheese has melted. (You will find that rolling them in salt has made the skin lovely and crisp.)

FRANKFURTERS IN BLANKETS

Mrs Braithwaite made one or three dozen o' these last bonfire night, went down a treat they did too. What didn't go down so well was me nearly bein' chucked on the bonfire as the guy. Very nasty experience that was. Ooh-arr.

Serves 2–4 people

Utensils needed: Scissors, small baking sheet, small saucepan, pastry brush, 4 skewers, knife, oven-gloves.

Oven temperature: Gas mark 7, 425°F, 220°C. Before you collect the ingredients, ask a grown-up to light the oven for you and to make sure there is a shelf near the top of the oven for you to use.

Cooking time: 15 minutes.

Ingredients:
    1 packet of 4 frankfurters
    4 slices of bread
    1 ounce (25g) butter or margarine
    a little mustard or tomato ketchup

Method:

Put the butter in the saucepan over a low heat, watching it carefully. Remove from the heat as soon as it has melted and set aside. Carefully open the packet of frankfurters with the scissors then place one on each slice of bread. Spread a little mustard or ketchup on them. Wrap the bread round the frankfurter and secure by putting a skewer right through the bread-wrapped frankfurter. Brush the bread with the melted butter, place on the baking sheet and bake for 15 minutes. When they are cooked remove them carefully from the oven, and transfer them to a serving dish. Eat while nice and hot.

CHEESE KEBABS

For the h'iggerent ones amongst you who don't know anythin', I'll tell you what a kebab is. It's bits o' food stuck on a pitchfork for us scarecrows. You yumans would use a skewer.

Serves 4 people

Utensils needed: Chopping board, knife, 4 skewers, 4 plates.

Ingredients:
- 8 ounces (225g) cheddar cheese – chopped into cubes
- 3 firm tomatoes – wiped clean and cut into quarters
- 8 radishes – trimmed and washed
- $\frac{1}{4}$ of a cucumber – wiped and cut into chunks
- 8 lettuce leaves – washed and patted dry with kitchen paper or a clean tea towel
- 1 tablespoon per person mayonnaise or salad cream
- potato crisps

Method:

Carefully push the cubes of cheese, the quarters of tomato, radishes and cucumber chunks on to the skewers. Make sure there are the same number of pieces on each skewer, and arrange them so that you don't get two things the same next to each other.

Put two lettuce leaves on every plate, place a kebab on the lettuce, add a blob of mayonnaise and a few potato crisps to finish it off.

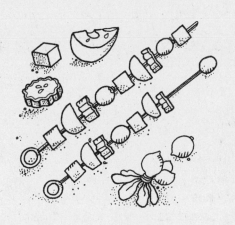

The filled skewer

FARMHOUSE BAKED BREAKFAST

Mrs Braithwaite, she cooks this for 'er 'usband an' 'Arry to eat when they comes in from mornin' milkin'. Course, if she should 'appen to turn 'er back for a minute to hang out 'er washin' or summat like that, then in I slips an' scoffs the lot. Ooh-arr!

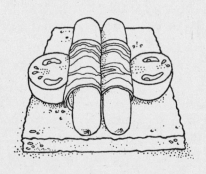

The finished breakfast should look like this

Serves 4 yumans or one Worzel

Utensils needed: Large baking sheet, chopping board, knife, kitchen scissors, oven-gloves, fish slice, 4 plates.

Oven temperature: Gas mark 6, 400°F, 200°C. Before you collect the ingredients, ask a grown-up to light the oven for you and to make sure there is a shelf just above the centre for you to use.

Cooking time: 25 minutes

Ingredients:
   8 chipolata sausages
   4 rashers streaky bacon
   4 tomatoes – wiped and cut in half
   4 slices of bread
   butter or margarine

Method:
   Using the kitchen scissors cut off the rind and remove any bone from the bacon rashers. Cut the rashers across into two and wrap each bacon half around a sausage. Trim the crusts off the bread, spread the slices with butter or margarine, place them butter side down on the baking sheet, and around a sausage. Trim the crusts off the bread, Put a tomato half, cut side uppermost, either side

19

of the sausages. Carefully put the baking sheet into the oven and bake for 25 minutes. When the time is up, wearing oven-gloves, carefully take the baking sheet out of the oven and, using a fish slice, put one piece of bread, sausages, bacon and tomatoes on a warmed plate and serve.

MUSHROOMS IN TOMATO CUPS

There's allus plenty o' mushrooms goin' beggin' in the meadow down Foggy Bottom – providin' you gets there early enough. An' there's allus plenty o' tomatoes goin' free in the greenhouse at Bloomsbury-Barton Hall – providin' you gets there afore Mrs Bloomsbury-Barton.

Serves 2 people

Utensils needed: Chopping board, knife, kitchen paper, small bowl, teaspoon, small baking sheet, oven-gloves, tongs.

Oven temperature: Gas mark 7, 425°F, 220°C. Before you collect the ingredients ask a grown-up to light the oven for you and to make sure there is a shelf just above the centre for you to use.

Cooking time: 10–15 minutes.

Ingredients:
   2 large tomatoes – wiped clean
   3 mushrooms
   Worcester sauce
   salt and pepper
   ½ ounce (15g) soft margarine

Method:
   Damp a piece of kitchen paper with water and wipe the mushrooms clean with it, then chop them finely and put them into the bowl. Cut the tops off the tomatoes, put them to one side and then carefully scoop out the insides. Chop these insides up and add them to the mushrooms. Season with a little salt, pepper, and a few drops of Worcester sauce. Put in the margarine, mix well and pack the mixture into the empty tomatoes. Replace the 'lids', stand the tomatoes on a lightly oiled baking sheet and bake for 10–15 minutes. Remove the cups carefully from the oven; if they are cooked enough they should 'give' a little when gently squeezed. Serve with cold, cooked meat, or on their own as a snack with toast or bread and butter.

HARVEST SLICES

*'Arry the farm 'and likes one or three o' these slices
to munch on when they're gettin' in the wheat in
Ten Acre Field. While 'ee's tendin' the combine
'arvester, I'm tendin' to what's in 'Arry's lunch-
box.*

Makes 10 slices

Utensils needed: Large bowl, small saucepan, grater, large spoon, fork, baking tin measuring 11″
×7″ × ¾″ (28 × 18 × 2cm), knife, oven-gloves,
serving dish.

Oven temperature: Gas mark 4, 350°F, 180°C.
Before you collect the ingredients, ask a
grown-up to light the oven for you and make
sure there is a shelf just above the centre for
you to use.

Cooking time: 20–25 minutes.

Ingredients:

- 5 ounces (150g) rolled oats
- 6 ounces (175g) carrots – washed, scraped and finely grated
- 4 ounces (100g) cheese – finely grated
- 1 egg
- 2 ounces (50g) block margarine
- salt and pepper
- 1 teaspoon Worcester sauce

Method:

Put the oats, carrots, cheese, a little salt and pepper and the Worcester sauce into the bowl. Melt the margarine in the saucepan over a low heat and add that to the mixture in the bowl. Crack the egg into a cup, beat it with a fork and pour it into the bowl. Mix the ingredients very thoroughly. Grease the baking tin with a little cooking oil then put the mixture in it, using a fork to spread it evenly. Carefully place the tin in the oven and bake for 20–25 minutes or until lightly browned on top. Remove the tin from the oven and allow to cool slightly before cutting into slices and transferring them to a serving dish. They can be eaten warm or cold.

COLD CUCUMBER SOUP

There's nothin' nicer, after an 'ot mornin' scarin' crows, than a cool, refreshin' bowl o' Cold Cucumber Soup.

Serves 2–3 people

Utensils needed: Chopping board, medium-sized bowl, measuring spoons, 2 knives – one sharp, one with a rounded end, wooden spoon, whisk.

Ingredients:
   1½ tablespoons oil – corn oil or any vegetable oil will do
   ¼ level teaspoon salt
   pepper
   ½ clove garlic
   ½ pint (3dl) plain yoghourt
   ½ cucumber
   ½ ounce (15g) chopped nuts – walnuts, peanuts, or almonds are especially good with this.
   a little chopped chives

Method:

First peel the cucumber and cut it into tiny cubes. Remove the skin from the garlic, place it on the board, sprinkle it with a tiny amount of salt, hold the end of the rounded knife firmly over the garlic, then bang your fist down on the knife, so crushing the garlic. Put the oil, salt, a little pepper and garlic into the bowl. Blend with the wooden spoon then whisk it for a moment. Whisk in the yoghourt and gently stir in the cucumber cubes. Chill in the fridge for about 30 minutes. When you are ready to serve, sprinkle on the nuts and chives. This soup tastes good with salted biscuits.

MRS BRAITHWAITE'S PICNIC FOOD

Sometimes Mrs Braithwaite packs the kids up with a picknic an' sends 'em off for a long walk in the country. But they don't never get no further than Ten Acre Field. T'aint my fault iffen while they're playing 'ide an' seek, their sangwiches decides to vanish good an' proper!

Each recipe contains enough ingredients to fill one sandwich.

Utensils needed: Bread board, measuring spoons, 2 knives, small and medium-sized bowls, fork, grater.

EGG AND BACON SANDWICHES

Ingredients:
   1 hard-boiled egg
   1 slice cold, crisply-cooked bacon
   1 dessertspoon mayonnaise
   ¼ teaspoon made mustard
   salt and pepper
   2 slices buttered bread

Method:
Chop the egg, crumble the bacon and put them together into a bowl with the mayonnaise, mustard, and a little salt and pepper. Mix thoroughly with a fork. Spread the mixture on one slice of bread and cover with the other slice. Cut into quarters.

HAM AND CHEESE SPREAD

Ingredients:
    1 tablespoon cooked ham – very finely chopped
    ½ ounce (15g) cheddar cheese – finely grated
    1 teaspoon tomato ketchup
    2 slices buttered bread

Method:
Put all the ingredients, except the bread, into a bowl and mix thoroughly with a wooden spoon. Spread on one slice of bread and cover with the other. Cut into quarters.

Sandwiches can be made with brown or white bread, but brown bread usually tastes more interesting. Crispbread or crackers can be used if the filling isn't too sloppy. Wrap sandwiches in greaseproof paper or plastic film to stop them getting dry.

Crisps are fun on any picnic. Cleaned, raw vegetables, such as carrots, radishes or celery, are a nice crunchy extra, and a lump of cucumber is cool and refreshing. Always remember to pack some salt in a twist of paper.

Don't put in anything too sticky if you want something sweet to eat as well. Try a couple of *Sunday Scones* (page 102) filled with jam or honey, or a few *Sugar Jumbles* (page 92) or *Gingery Biskits* (page 73), which are easy to pack and eat. Add a piece of fruit and, of course, don't forget a delicious drink. Here's a suggestion for one you can make yourself.

PICNIC PUNCH

Makes about ½ pint (3dl)

Utensils needed: Orange squeezer, sieve, jug, spoon, thermos flask or wide-necked plastic bottle.

Ingredients:
  2 large oranges
  1 teaspoon lemon juice – the bottled kind will
    do
  ¼ pint (1½dl) water
  sugar to taste
  ice cubes

Method:

Squeeze the oranges and strain the juice through the sieve into the jug. Add the lemon juice, water and a couple of teaspoons of sugar. Stir with the spoon until the sugar dissolves. Taste to see if it needs any more sugar. Chill in a fridge for at least an hour, then pour into a thermos or container with several ice cubes.

EASY CHEESY PUFFS

These tasty titbits is what that ol' baggage Mrs Bloomsbury-Barton gives to 'er guests when she 'as 'em in of an evenin' for a drink. Last time I tried to invite meself round, 'er butler kicked me out an' called me a 'gate-crasher'. Danged liar! Only time I ever crashed into a gate was when I got chased by Farmer Braithwaite's bull. Mind you, I wouldn't mind bashin' into 'alf a dozen gates for a few o' these 'ere puffs.

Makes about 30 puffs

Utensils needed: Large baking sheet, large bowl, wooden spoon, fish slice, kitchen paper, plate, oven-gloves, grater.

Oven temperature: Gas mark 5, 375°F, 190°C. Before you mix the ingredients, ask a grown-up to light the oven for you and to make sure there is a shelf near the top of the oven for you to use.

Cooking Time: 10–15 minutes.

Ingredients:
   1½ ounces (40g) plain flour
   3 ounces (75g) cheese – finely grated
   1½ ounces (40g) butter – don't use butter
      straight from the fridge, as it should be
      slightly soft
   pinch of salt
   pinch of dry mustard
   pinch of paprika

Method:
Grease the baking sheet with some buttered
paper. Place the butter in the bowl and soften it
with the wooden spoon. Stir in the grated cheese
until it is well blended with the butter. Add the
flour, salt, mustard and paprika. Mix thoroughly
until all the ingredients start to stick together in a
large lump. Use your hands to form the mixture
into a ball. Put a little flour in your hands, pull off
little pieces of mixture and roll them into balls the
size of marbles. Place them on the baking sheet
about 1½ inches (4cm) apart. When the mixture is
used up, carefully put the cheesy puffs into the
oven and cook for 10–15 minutes, or until they
are a little brown around the edge and golden in
the centre. Remove the baking sheet from the
oven, using the oven-gloves. Put some crumpled
kitchen paper on the plate and, using the fish

slice, transfer the puffs from the baking sheet to the paper.

Easy cheesy puffs taste good with a hot beefy drink, or a cup of soup.

SAVOURY PEARS

That fat ol' barrel o' lard, Mrs Bloomsbury-Barton, eats this for 'er lunch when she's watchin' 'er weight. But iffen she ain't watchin' 'er kitchen door, I nips in an' eats them pears first. Just 'elping 'er keep down 'er calories an' all.

Serves 2 people

Utensils needed: Chopping board, pastry brush, grater, medium-sized bowl, teaspoon, knife, wooden spoon, 2 plates.

Ingredients:
  1 ripe pear
  1 tablespoon lemon juice – the bottled sort will do
  1 eating apple or 1 stick of celery
  mayonnaise or salad cream
  3 ounces (75g) cream cheese
  1 tablespoon chopped walnuts
  2 large lettuce leaves – washed and patted dry on some kitchen paper

Method:

Peel the pear, cut it in half lengthways, then remove the core using the teaspoon. There should be a nice hole left in each half to hold the filling. Now dip the pastry brush in the lemon juice and brush the pears all over with lemon (this stops them from becoming discoloured). Either finely chop the celery, or chop or grate the apple. Put the cheese into the bowl and soften it with the wooden spoon, then blend in 2 or 3 teaspoons of mayonnaise or salad cream. Now add the apple or celery and mix well. Fill the pear halves with the creamy mixture, place a lettuce leaf on each plate and put a pear half on top. Sprinkle with chopped walnuts, then chill in the fridge for 20 minutes before serving. This makes a good lunchtime snack, eaten with thinly sliced brown bread and butter.

STUFFED TOMATOES

*I throwed one o' these at P.C. Parsons t'other day.
It 'it 'im on the nose an' made 'im fall off 'is bike.
When I'm not throwing 'em, I stuffs 'em down a
rare ol' treat.*

Serves 4 people

Utensils needed: Chopping board, knife, teaspoon, small saucepan, fork, cup, wooden
spoon, grater, medium-sized bowl, 4 plates.

Ingredients:
  4 tomatoes – wiped clean and with stalks
     removed
  ¾ ounce (20g) butter or margarine
  1 egg
  1 tablespoon of milk
  1 level teaspoon chives – these are not essen-
     tial, but if you do have some, wash them and
     snip them into little bits with kitchen scissors
  4 ounces (100g) cheddar cheese – grated
  1 tablespoon salad cream
  4 slices bread and butter
  salt and pepper

Method:

Cut a little slice from the rounded end of each tomato and set these slices aside. Carefully scoop out the pulp with a teaspoon. Chop the pulp and put it in the bowl. Crack the eggs into the cup and beat them lightly with the fork. Melt the butter in the pan over a medium heat, pour in the eggs and the milk, and cook gently, stirring with a wooden spoon, until the mixture starts to set or 'scramble'. Put this mixture into the bowl with the tomato pulp, add the chives, cheese, salad cream, and a little salt and pepper. Mix well, then leave until cold. Put spoonfuls of the filling into the tomatoes and replace the 'caps' you sliced off in the beginning. Place a tomato on each plate, cut the bread and butter into triangles and arrange them around the tomatoes.

MOCK SOUFFLÉ

Crowman baked this once for me an' Soggy Bog-gart an' Earthy Mangold an' one or three other scarecrows. Good 'olesome cookin' don't mean much to the likes o' them – they'd rather 'ave a bucket o' pig-swill any Tuesday o' the week.

Serves 4 people

Utensils needed: Chopping board, knife, a 1-pint size (6dl) ovenproof dish, grater, medium-sized bowl, fork, measuring jug, oven-gloves.

Oven temperature: Gas mark 5, 375°F, 190°C. While you leave the mixture to soak, ask a grown-up to light the oven for you and to make sure there is a shelf in the centre for you to use.

Cooking time: 30–35 minutes.

Ingredients:

2 slices of buttered bread
4 ounces (100g) cheese – finely grated
2 eggs
salt and pepper
½ teaspoon English mustard – the ready-made kind
½ pint (3dl) milk

Method:

First grease the ovenproof dish with a little butter or margarine. Trim the crusts off the bread and cut the slices into cubes. Place the cubes in the dish so they cover the bottom evenly. Put one tablespoon of the cheese to one side and sprinkle the rest over the bread cubes. Crack the eggs into the bowl, add the milk, a little salt and pepper and mustard, then beat well with the fork. Pour this over the bread and leave to soak for 30 minutes. When the time is up, sprinkle the remaining tablespoon of cheese over the bread. Bake the Mock Soufflé in the oven for 30–35 minutes or until it has puffed up and is firm and golden brown. Remove carefully from the oven and serve hot with baked beans, grilled or baked tomatoes, or peas.

EGG IN THE HOLE

Them two titchy yumans tol' me they 'ad to go 'ome 'cos they 'ad toad in the 'ole for supper. Pussonally speakin' I don't like eatin' anythin' that's green an' slippery, but a nice egg in the 'ole is an altogether different kettle o' tiddlers.

Serves 2 people

Utensils needed: Chopping board, knife, cup, spoon, small baking sheet, oven-gloves.

Oven temperature: Gas mark 4, 350°F, 180°C. Before you collect the ingredients, ask a grown-up to light the oven for you and to make sure there is a shelf in the centre for you to use.

Cooking time: 20–30 minutes.

Ingredients:
    2 large crisp rolls
    2 eggs
    ½ ounce (15g) butter or margarine
    salt and pepper

Method:

Stand the rolls on the board and cut a slice off the top of each one, so making a lid. Scoop out some of the soft inside of the rolls, then butter the insides and the lids. Break an egg into a cup then carefully slide it into the roll. Repeat with the other egg. Season with just a little salt and pepper, replace the lids, place the rolls on the baking sheet and bake them for 20–30 minutes or until the eggs are set but not hard. They can be eaten hot or cold. To vary this recipe blend the butter with a tiny amount of yeast extract and use on the inside of the rolls, or place a slice of tomato in the roll before adding the egg, season but don't replace the lid, just sprinkle some grated cheese on top.

*A VERY HEALTHY SALAD

Mebbe you knows that I 'appens to 'ave a gard'nin' 'ead. Very fond o' growin' vegetaters it is – an' even fonder o' eatin' 'em.

Serves 2–3 people

Utensils needed: Chopping board, knife, a large bowl that looks attractive enough to serve from, 2 large spoons.

Ingredients:
   1 eating apple – wiped clean
   1 small onion – skin removed
   1 medium-sized carrot – washed, pared, and grated
   $\frac{1}{4}$ of a white cabbage – washed and dried on a kitchen paper
   1 tablespoon of lemon juice – the bottled kind will do
   a handful of currants or raisins
   a handful of chopped nuts
   mayonnaise or french dressing

Method:

Remove any thick stalk from the cabbage quarter then shred it as finely as you can. Chop the onion into small pieces. Put the lemon juice into the bowl, then cut the apple into quarters, remove the core, chop the rest of the apple up small, leaving the skin on, and add it to the lemon juice. Toss it about in the juice to coat it well and to stop it from discolouring. Now add the cabbage, carrot, onion, fruit and nuts. Mix together thoroughly. Dress the salad with enough mayonnaise or French dressing to make it moist. Serve the salad from the bowl with some crusty bread.

FRENCH DRESSING

Utensils needed: Measuring spoons, screw-top jar.

Ingredients:
1 tablespoon wine or tarragon vinegar
$\frac{1}{2}$ teaspoon of salt
$\frac{1}{2}$ teaspoon of pepper – freshly ground black pepper if possible
3 tablespoons of salad oil

Method:

Put the vinegar, salt and pepper into the jar, swirl them round so that they blend together. Now add the oil, screw on the lid tightly and shake the jar vigorously while you count slowly to ten. By the time you have finished counting, the dressing should have thickened. Store this dressing in the fridge and always give it a good shake just before you use it.

WORZEL'S PINK DIP

This tastes better than that dang dratted sheep dip I fell into year before last.

Serves 4–6 people

Utensils needed: 2 medium-sized bowls, measuring spoons, wooden spoon, serving bowl.

Ingredients:
   2 × 3 ounce (75g) packets of cream cheese
      spread
   1 dessertspoon salad cream
   1 tablespoon tomato ketchup
   salt
   potato crisps or little savoury biscuits

Method:

Take the cream cheese out of the fridge an hour before you need to use it. This makes it easier to soften. Blend the salad cream and tomato ketchup together in a bowl. Put the cream cheese in another bowl and cream it with the wooden spoon until it is soft and smooth. This will be quite hard work. Now gradually work the salad cream mixture into the cheese. Add a pinch of salt, mix thoroughly and turn the dip into a serving bowl. Serve with potato crisps, savoury biscuits, or raw vegetables, like carrots and celery, washed and cut into short lengths.

TOMATO AND CHEESE HOT POT

Mrs Braithwaite's been givin' that titchy yuman, Sue, cookery lessons. She should o' knowed better an' come to me for 'em seein' as 'ow I'm the expert. Anywise, she once made this 'ot pot for 'er dad's an' 'er brother's supper. On 'er way to the caravan she stops by the barn an' axes my opinion — course, I 'ave to 'ave three or five platefuls afore I makes up my mind.

Serves 4 people

Utensils needed: Chopping board, knife, grater, medium-sized casserole, measuring spoons, flat dish, potato masher, oven-gloves.

Oven temperature: Gas mark 4, 350°F, 180°C. Before you collect the ingredients ask a grown-up to light the oven for you and to make sure there is a shelf in the centre for you to use.

Cooking time: 30 minutes.

Ingredients:

4 medium-sized tomatoes – cut into ½ inch (1cm) thick slices

4 ounces (100g) cheese – grated

1 small onion – skinned and thinly sliced

½ teaspoon salt

⅛ teaspoon pepper

2 ounces (50g) potato crisps

Method:

Lightly grease the inside of the casserole with a little butter or margarine. Put the crisps onto a flat dish and crush them with the potato masher. Cover the bottom of the casserole with half the tomato slices. Season with a little salt and pepper. Make a second layer with half the cheese and onion. Now repeat this procedure with the remaining tomatoes, onion and cheese, not forgetting to season the tomatoes. Sprinkle the potato crisps over the top. Cook in the oven for 30 minutes or until the cheese has melted and is bubbly. This can be eaten on its own as a hot snack with some crusty bread, or as a vegetable dish with sausages or chops.

SCARECROWS' FINGERS

You yumans call these cheese straws, but seein' 'as 'ow the Crowman made my 'ands out o' straw, I calls 'em scarecrows' fingers.
Makes about 50 fingers.

Utensils needed: Large bowl, 2 knives, teaspoon, rolling pin, pastry board, large baking sheet, fish slice, sieve, oven-gloves, cooling rack.

Oven temperature: Gas mark 6, 400°F, 200°C. Before you start making the pastry, ask a grown-up to light the oven for you and make sure there is a shelf near the top of the oven for you to use.

Cooking time: 8–10 minutes.

Ingredients:
  3 ounces (75g) plain flour
  pinch of salt
  ¾ ounce (20g) lard
  ¾ ounce (20g) margarine – the hard kind
  1½ ounces (40g) cheddar cheese – finely grated
  4–6 teaspoons cold water

Method:

Sift the flour and salt into the bowl, then put in the lard and margarine. Take a knife in each hand and, using a criss-cross scissor action, cut the fat into little pieces that are well coated with flour. Take handfuls of the mixture and rub it between your thumbs and fingertips as you let it fall back into the bowl. Repeat this until it looks like breadcrumbs. Sprinkle in about 4 teaspoons of water and stir the mixture with a knife until it sticks together in little lumps. If it seems dry and crumbly add a little more water. When the lumps get bigger use your hand to knead the pastry into

Rub in the fat between your fingers and thumbs

a smooth ball. Turn the pastry onto a floured board, flour the rolling pin then roll the pastry into a thin rectangle that measures approximately 12 × 9 inches (30½ × 23cm). Trim the edges with a knife, then cut out narrow strips, about ¼ inch (½cm) wide and 4 or 5 inches (10 or 12½cm) long, and place them on an ungreased baking sheet. Roll out any trimmings and cut these into straws or fingers. Carefully put them into the oven and bake for 8–10 minutes, or until they are just golden. Transfer them to the cooling rack with the fish slice. When cold store them in an airtight tin.

*SCARECROW'S SOOPER SOUP

Me an' the Crowman, we likes a drop o' this 'ere soup on a cold evenin' in Ten Acre Field.

Serves 4 people

Utensils needed: Chopping board, potato peeler, knife, 2 jugs, cheese grater, medium-sized saucepan, 4 soup bowls.

Ingredients:
    1 large potato – peeled and cut into cubes
    1 large onion – peeled and chopped up small
    1 medium-sized carrot – scraped and cut up small
    1 stick of celery – washed and cut up small
    1 pint chicken stock – made with a chicken stock cube and a pint (6dl) of boiling water. You must ask a grown-up to prepare this for you.
    $\frac{1}{4}$ lb (100g) strong cheddar cheese – grated
    $\frac{1}{4}$ pint (1$\frac{1}{2}$dl) creamy milk
    salt and pepper

Method:

Put the potato, onion, carrot and celery into the saucepan, then carefully pour on the stock. Place the saucepan over a low to moderate heat and let the soup simmer – that means to cook slowly so the liquid bubbles gently in the centre – for 20–25 minutes. Now put in the cheese and milk. Let the soup heat through for another 5 minutes but don't let it boil. Season with a little salt and pepper. Serve in warmed soup bowls with chunks of bread.

WORZELADE

T'other scarecrows allus asks for Worzel's aid when it comes to mixin' drinks at the Scarecrows' Ball – 'cos Worzelade's the favourite drink o' scarecrows.

Makes 1½ pints (9dl)

Utensils needed: Large jug, chopping board, knife, orange squeezer, wooden spoon, strainer, large bowl pretty enough to serve from.

Ingredients:
   7 ounces (200g) granulated sugar
   ½ pint (3dl) hot water
   2 lemons
   2 oranges
   2 grapefruits

Method:

First ask a grown-up to boil some water for you. Once it has boiled get them to set it aside for five minutes to cool down a little. Now pour ½ pint (3dl) of the hot water into the jug, add the sugar and stir with the wooden spoon until it has dissolved. Set aside to allow the liquid to cool some more. Cut all the fruit in half and, using the orange squeezer, extract as much juice from the fruit as you can. Pour the juice through the strainer into the bowl as you go along. When the sugar water is really cool add it to the fruit juice, stir to mix and put the bowl into the fridge to chill. If you can, serve this with some slices of fresh fruit in it, or cherries frozen in ice cubes to make it really special.

WORZEL'S MUESLI

Some mornin's my stummick feels emptier than it does on t'other mornin's. Iffen it does, I goes into the farmyard early afore them yumans start clatterin' about. I fills meself a bucketful o' this 'ere moosly, takes it into the cowshed an' ol' Daisy tops it up wi' milk.

Makes several helpings

Utensils needed: Chopping board, knife, large bowl, large spoon, storage jar or airtight tin.

Ingredients:
    12 ounces (350g) porridge oats or rolled oats
    2 or 3 ounces (50–75g) soft brown sugar
    3 ounces (75g) raisins
    3 ounces (75g) sultanas
    1 or 2 ounces (25–50g) dried apricots – chopped up small
    ½ ounce (15g) hazelnuts or walnuts
    ½–1 ounce (15–25g) bran – this is optional

Method:

Place all the ingredients, except the sugar, into the bowl. Start by adding only 2 ounces (50g) of the sugar, then when you have mixed it together you can taste the muesli to see if you need to add the extra ounce (25g). Mix everything thoroughly, then transfer it to a jar or airtight tin. You can vary the ingredients according to your own taste, adding more or less fruit and nuts. The night before you intend eating it, place a portion in a cereal bowl and pour on just enough milk to cover the muesli. In the morning just stir and eat. Grated apple, sliced banana or stewed fruits taste good with this.

CHOCOLATE CRUNCH CAKES

There's one sure way o' gettin' me out o' a long sulk, an' that's to offer me a chocolate crunch cake.

Makes 6–8 cakes

Utensils needed: Medium-sized saucepan, 2 tablespoons, wooden spoon, teaspoon, paper cases.

Ingredients:
   1 ounce (25g) butter or margarine
   1 tablespoon icing sugar
   1 tablespoon syrup
   1 tablespoon cocoa powder
   7–8 tablespoons cornflakes

Method:

When you measure your ingredients, use one tablespoon for the dry ingredients and the other spoon for the syrup.

Put the butter or margarine in the saucepan over a low heat and let it melt. Add the icing sugar, syrup and cocoa powder, stirring it all with a wooden spoon until the mixture becomes smooth and chocolaty. Remove the pan from the heat, making sure you stand it on a heat-proof surface, and stir in the cornflakes. Do this gently but thoroughly, so that they are well coated in chocolate but not too broken up. Put a couple of teaspoonfuls of the chocolate-coated cornflakes into each paper case until they are all used up. If you put the paper cases in a bun tin it will stop them from moving about while you fill them. Put the cakes in a cool place to set before you eat them.

This is one recipe where the measurements don't have to be exact: a little more cocoa or a few extra cornflakes won't spoil the end result. You can even experiment and add a few raisins or chopped nuts, or some glacé cherries cut up small. Just take out one tablespoonful of cornflakes and add a tablespoonful of an ingredient of your own choice.

JOHN AND·SUE'S HONEY MILK DRINK

Those two titchy yumans, John an' Sue, what lives in that caravan up at Scatterbrook, they 'as a smashin' tastin' milk drink afore they goes to bed. They sometimes shares it with ol' Worzel, but I can't drink it inside the caravan 'cos that pesky dad o' theirs don't like findin' straw an' twigs all over 'is furniture.

Makes 2 or 3 mugs

Utensils needed: Medium-sized saucepan, wooden spoon, measuring-spoons, 2 or 3 mugs.

Ingredients:
 ¾ pint (4dl) milk
 ¼ teaspoon vanilla essence
 2 tablespoons clear honey
 ground cinnamon

Method:

Heat the milk in the saucepan over a medium heat until bubbles appear around the edge. Do not let it boil. Using the wooden spoon, stir in the vanilla essence and honey. Carefully pour the milk into 2 or 3 mugs, sprinkle a little cinnamon over each drink and serve.

BLACKCURRANT SUNDAE

It's daft namin' this after a day o' the week, 'cos if you wants to you could call it after any day o' the year. I'd call it Blackcurrant Fortnight.

Makes enough for one person

Utensils needed: Small bowl – with a lip if possible, tablespoon, rotary whisk, tall glass.

Ingredients:
   $\frac{1}{4}$ pint (1$\frac{1}{2}$dl) milk – straight from the fridge
   2 tablespoons blackcurrant syrup or cordial
   1 small portion of vanilla ice cream – remove
      this from the fridge a little while before you
      want to use it as it should not be too hard.

Method:
   Put the milk and the blackcurrant syrup into the bowl. Add the ice cream. Ask your mother to show you how to use the rotary whisk if you don't already know, and then beat the mixture with the whisk until frothy. Pour into the glass and serve with a straw.

Beat the mixture with a rotary whisk

BANANA AND HONEY TOAST

The 'edgehog as I combs my 'air with is partial to a nibble o' this at tea-time — but if I shares it with the robin in my stummick, she turns 'er beak up 'cos it makes her nest all sticky.

Serves 4 people

Utensils needed: Chopping board or bread board, medium-sized bowl, fork, knife, fish slice, grill pan, 4 plates.

Ingredients:
   2 ripe bananas
   1 teaspoon lemon juice
   1 tablespoon clear honey
   4 slices bread
   butter or margarine

Method:

First ask a grown-up to light the grill for you while you prepare the spread for the toast. Peel the bananas, put them in the bowl and mash them well with the fork. Now mix in the lemon juice and the honey. Put the bread on the grill pan, put the pan under the grill, and toast the bread on both sides. Spread one side of the toast with butter or margarine, and the banana spread. Put the slices back under the grill for about 2 minutes, or until the banana mixture starts to sizzle. Remove the grill pan from the heat, and use the fish slice to put the banana and honey toast on to the plates. You can also sprinkle a few chopped walnuts over the top if you like.

*GINGERY BISKITS

I knows an ol' squirrel, who gives me a lend o' 'is tail sometimes for a clothes brush. 'E 'as a sweet tooth for a gingery biskit too. Stores them away, 'e does, with 'is winter nuts.

Makes about 16 biscuits.

Utensils needed: Large baking sheet, large bowl, knife, measuring spoons, sieve, wooden spoon, oven-gloves, cooling rack.

Oven temperature: Gas mark 5, 375°F, 190°C. Before you collect the ingredients, ask a grown-up to light the oven for you and to make sure there is a shelf just above the centre for you to use.

Cooking time: 15–20 minutes.

Ingredients:
    4 ounces (110g) self-raising flour
    1 slightly rounded teaspoon ground ginger
    1 level teaspoon bicarbonate of soda
    1½ ounces (40g) granulated sugar
    2 ounces (50g) block margarine – cut into small
        pieces
    2 tablespoons golden syrup

Method:
First grease the baking sheet with a little cooking oil, then set it aside. Sieve the flour, ground
ginger and bicarbonate of soda into the bowl,
then add the sugar and margarine pieces. Pick up
handfuls of fat and flour and rub it with your
fingertips as you let it trickle back into the bowl.
This is called 'rubbing in', and you repeat this
until the mixture looks like breadcrumbs. Now
add the syrup and mix everything with the
wooden spoon until the mixture forms a stiff
paste. Divide the mixture into 16 even-sized
pieces, roll them into little balls and place them
on the baking sheet. Leave plenty of space between the biscuits, as they spread during cooking.
Flatten them a little and bake them for 15–20
minutes, or until they are golden brown and the
surface looks cracked. Carefully remove them

from the oven and let them cool on the baking sheet for 10 minutes before transferring them to a cooling rack. When they are cold store them in an airtight tin.

AUNT SALLY'S APPLE FOOL

I made this puddin' speshul for Aunt Sally, but instead o' eatin' it she threw it at me an' called me a stewpid fool. Still it only goes to show 'ow much she loves me (I 'opes).

Serves four people

Utensils needed: Plastic bag, wooden board, rolling pin, medium-sized bowl, measuring spoons, small saucepan, wooden spoon, 4 glass dessert bowls or 4 clear-plastic cartons.

Ingredients:
1 packet dehydrated apple flakes (ask your mother to buy this for you at a supermarket or health food shop)
½ pint (3dl) water
2 small cartons plain yoghourt
4 teaspoons clear honey
4 digestive biscuits

Method:

Put the water and the apple flakes in the saucepan over a medium heat. Bring to the boil, stirring with the wooden spoon, turn the heat to low and cook for one minute. Turn the apple into a bowl and leave until cold. This will probably take at least two hours, and, as with all hot things, you mustn't put it in the fridge.

When the apple is quite cold, add the two cartons of yoghourt and the honey, and mix together well. Put the biscuits in the plastic bag, place the bag on the board and crush the biscuits into fine

Roll the biscuits in the bag into crumbs

crumbs using the rolling pin. Put one tablespoon of apple into each dish or carton, then add a thick layer of biscuit crumbs. Put in another layer of apple, finishing it up this time, then sprinkle the remaining crumbs on top. Let the apple fool chill for at least an hour in the fridge before serving.

CROWMAN'S SPECIAL COCOA

Every evenin' the Crowman makes 'imself a nice cuppa cocoa, an' if I 'appens to be passing 'is cottage roundabout then 'is 'ighness sometimes asks me to join 'im. It's funny 'as 'ow he always 'as enough for two cups!

Makes enough for two full mugs

Utensils needed: Medium-sized saucepan, large jug, rotary whisk, teaspoon, wooden spoon, 2 mugs.

Ingredients:
  2 level teaspoons cocoa powder
  4 level teaspoons sugar
  $\frac{3}{4}$ pint (4dl) milk

Method:

Place the cocoa and sugar in the jug, stir it into a smooth paste with a little of the milk. Heat the rest of the milk in the saucepan over a medium heat until bubbles appear around the edge. Carefully pour the milk into the cocoa. Whisk thoroughly for 30 seconds. Pour the cocoa into two mugs and serve.

BREAD AND BUTTER PUDDING

That ol' baggage Mrs Bloomsbury-Barton, she b'aint no good at cookin' so she 'as to get another yuman to do it for 'er. This 'ere cook-woman can make a better bread an' butter puddin' than me but she can't run faster than what I does.

Serves 4 people

Utensils needed: Chopping board or bread board, 2 knives, medium-sized bowl, rotary whisk, medium-sized ovenproof dish, oven-gloves.

Oven temperature: Gas mark 4, 350°F, 180°C. When you leave the mixture to soak, ask a grown-up to light the oven for you and to make sure there is a shelf in the centre for you to use.

Cooking time: 35–40 minutes.

Ingredients:
   4 or 5 slices of stale brown bread
   some butter or margarine
   some marmalade or jam
   1 ounce (25g) soft brown sugar
   ¾ pint (4dl) milk
   2 eggs

Method:
Trim the crusts off the bread, butter the slices and spread them with jam or marmalade. Grease the ovenproof dish with a little butter or margarine. Cut the bread into fingers and arrange them, jam side up, in the bottom of the dish. Sprinkle them with the sugar. Crack the eggs into

Arrange the bread fingers in the bottom of the dish

the bowl, pour in the milk and beat this thoroughly with the whisk. Pour the mixture over the bread. Ask a grown-up to light the oven for you, and then leave the mixture to soak for 20 minutes.

When the 20 minutes is up, place the pudding in the oven and bake for 35–40 minutes, or until the custard has set. Serve while hot.

NO-NEED-TO-BAKE CHOCOLATE CAKE

*As you probably knows, chocolate cake is my
favourite cake. An' it's not only my favourite cake
to eat, it's my favourite cake to make an' all. You
don't need no oven to bake it in — all you need is a
couple o' bunches o' twigs, or 'ands.*

Makes one cake

Utensils needed: Large bowl, large plate, wooden
board, rolling pin, plastic bag, wooden spoon,
tablespoon, small saucepan, 7½ or 8½ inch (19
or 21½cm) loose-bottomed cake tin, knife,
sieve.

Ingredients:
  6 ounces (175g) assorted sweet biscuits (you
    can include digestive biscuits, and even some
    cornflakes or rice crispies)
  2 ounces (50g) shelled walnuts
  3½ ounces (90g) soft margarine
  1 ounce (25g) caster sugar
  3 tablespoons golden syrup
  2 ounces (50g) cocoa powder

For the icing:
2 ounces (50g) cooking chocolate
1 tablespoon hot water
2½ ounces (65g) icing sugar – sifted
knob of butter

Method:
Put a handful of the biscuits and walnuts into
the plastic bag, place the bag on the board and
crush them with the rolling pin. Roll the pin back
and forth over the bag, pressing down hard so
that the biscuits and nuts are reduced to small
pieces. Empty the bag on to the plate, then crush
the remaining biscuits in the same way. Put the
margarine, sugar and golden syrup into the large
bowl. Using the wooden spoon, blend them
together until the mixture becomes soft and light
in colour. Carefully stir in the cocoa, then work in
the biscuits and nuts. Make sure they are all well
coated with chocolate. Turn the mixture into the
ungreased cake tin, spreading it evenly with a
knife. Chill in the fridge overnight.

To make the icing:

First remove the cake from the cake tin (if you push it up from the bottom, it should come out quite easily). Put the chocolate, icing sugar, hot water and butter into the saucepan. Place it over a very low heat and stir until the chocolate has melted. Set it aside for 2 or 3 minutes to cool. Pour the icing onto the centre of the cake and spread it evenly with a knife dipped in hot water. Leave the icing to set for at least ten minutes before cutting the cake.

You can decorate the cake with more walnuts, grated chocolate, or glacé cherries.

CINNAMON TOAST

That dopey Mr Peters goes around fixin' other people's electrics. But when it comes to fixin' a piece o' toast for John an' Sue's tea he's worse than useless, judgin' by the 'orrible smell o' burnin' comin' from Mrs Braithwaite's kitchen. 'Ere's 'ow you can fix it proper.

Serves 2 people

Utensils needed: Knife, bread board, measuring spoons, small bowl, grill pan, fish slice, 2 plates.

Ingredients:
    1½ teaspoons ground cinnamon
    2 tablespoons brown sugar
    2 slices of bread
    butter or margarine

Method:

Ask a grown-up to light the grill for you while you collect the ingredients together. Mix the cinnamon and sugar together in a bowl. Toast the bread on both sides and spread one side with the butter or margarine and then sprinkle on the cinnamon sugar. Put the pan back under the grill for about 2 minutes or until the sugar has melted. Transfer the toast to the plates with the fish slice. Eat while hot.

SUGAR JUMBLES

I tried to enter these ere biskits for the village bakin' competishun. But that ol' faggot Mrs Bloomsbury-Barton wouldn't let me in the judgin' tent. I reckons she knows 'er rotten biskits didn't stand a chance against mine.

Makes about 30—36 Sugar Jumbles

Utensils needed: 1 medium-sized bowl, 1 large bowl, sieve, cup, measuring spoons, wooden spoon, fork, 2 teaspoons, oven-gloves, fish slice, cooling rack, 2–3 large baking sheets.

Oven temperature: Gas mark 5, 375°F, 190°C. Before you weigh out the ingredients, ask a grown-up to light the oven for you and to make sure there is a shelf just above the centre for you to use.

Cooking time: 8–12 minutes.

Ingredients:
- 4½ ounces (115g) plain flour
- ¼ teaspoon bicarbonate of soda
- ½ teaspoon salt
- 4 ounces (100g) soft margarine
- 4 ounces (100g) sugar
- 1 egg
- ½ teaspoon vanilla essence

Method:
Sift the flour, bicarbonate of soda, and salt into the medium-sized bowl. Put the margarine, sugar and vanilla into the large bowl. Break the egg into the cup and stir it lightly with the fork, then add it to the ingredients in the large bowl. Using a wooden spoon, stir these ingredients together thoroughly. Now tip in the flour and stir the mixture again until it is well blended.

Grease the baking sheets lightly with a little vegetable oil. Put rounded teaspoons of the mixture onto one of the sheets, keeping them at least 2 inches (5cm) apart as they spread quite a lot during cooking. When you have filled one baking sheet, carefully put it into the oven and cook the jumbles for 8–12 minutes, or until they are very pale brown. They should still be soft in the centre when you take them out of the oven. Let them cool slightly, then, using a fish slice, transfer the jumbles to a cooling rack. While the first batch is cooking, put the remaining mixture onto the other baking sheets. When the jumbles are cold, store them in an airtight tin.

*BAKED APPLES

Mrs Parsons, the policeman's wife, does a wunnerful baked apple. I oughter know, 'cos a couple of 'em came my way one time — an' this is 'ow it 'appened. She'd cooked 'em for 'er 'ubby's supper, but I'd let his bicycle tyres down, so she reckoned as 'ow 'e wasn't coming 'ome that night, an' slung 'is supper in the dustbin. Guess who was 'idin' round the corner of their garden shed, waitin' to see they wussn't wasted?

Serves 4 people

Utensils needed: Medium-sized ovenproof dish, chopping board, apple corer, knife, teaspoon, oven-gloves.

Oven temperature: Gas mark 6, 400°F, 200°C. Before you collect the ingredients, ask a grown-up to light the oven for you and to make sure there is a shelf in the centre of the oven for you to use.

Cooking time: 35–45 minutes.

Ingredients:
   4 even-sized cooking apples – washed and
      dried on kitchen paper
   3 ounces (75g) demerara sugar
   1 ounce (25g) butter
   ¾ pint (1½dl) water

Method:
Grease the ovenproof dish with a little cooking oil. Hold the apple, stalk end up, firmly on the
board. Put the corer over the stalk and push
downwards, twisting the corer as you go, until it

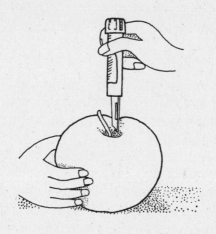

*Holding the apple firmly, push the corer through
the middle*

has gone right through the apple. Withdraw the corer, and you should have a nice clean hole through the centre of the apple. Throw away the core. Using the knife, make a cut right round the middle of the apple, piercing the skin, not the flesh. Repeat this with the other apples, then put them in the dish and fill the holes with the sugar, using the teaspoon. Place a knob of butter on the top of each. Pour the water in the dish round the apples, carefully place them in the oven and bake for 35–45 minutes, or until soft.

If you like, you can pop some sultanas or raisins into the middle of each apple, mixed in with the sugar, before placing the knob of butter on each apple.

*RAISIN POPOVERS

When Mrs Braithwaite bakes these, the smell o' them wafts out from her kitchen, drifts across Ten Acre Field, an' creeps up the nostrils o' my carrot nose. Soon as I gets a whiff o' them popovers, I straightways pops over to the farmhouse an' samples a few when no one's lookin'.

Makes 12—18 popovers

Utensils needed: Sieve, medium-sized bowl, wooden spoon, tablespoon, rotary whisk, 12-hole bun tin, jug, oven-gloves.

Oven temperatures: Gas mark 7, 425°F, 220°C. Before you collect the ingredients, ask a grown-up to light the oven for you and to make sure there is a shelf near the top of the oven for you to use.

Cooking time: 20–25 minutes.

Ingredients:
    4 ounces (100g) plain flour
    2 ounces (50g) caster sugar
    2 eggs
    ½ pint (3dl) milk
    2 ounces (50g) raisins

Method:
Grease the bun tin with some buttered paper.
Sieve the flour and sugar into the bowl, make a
well in the centre and break the eggs into it. Pour
in half the milk – ¼ pint (1½dl). Using the wooden
spoon, blend the flour into the egg and milk,
starting in the middle of the mixture and gradually
working outwards as the flour gets incorporated
into the liquid. Don't hurry this; the mixture
should be thick, smooth and fairly lump-free.
Now pour in the remaining milk and beat for one
whole minute with the rotary whisk. With a
grown-up's help, pour the batter through the sieve
into the jug, throwing away any bits left in the
sieve. Stir the raisins into the batter, then spoon it
into the bun tin, filling the holes up to halfway.
Bake them for 20–25 minutes, or until they have
risen or 'popped' and they are nice and brown.
Serve while hot with golden syrup.
    If you have some batter left in the jug you can
keep it in the fridge for a couple of days. Just give
it a good whizz with a whisk before using it.

Hold the sieve and bowl steady while a grown-up pours the batter

*SUNDAY SCONES

Every Sunday, reg'lar as clockwork, Mrs Braith-waite makes a batch o' scones an' leaves 'em on the winder-sill to cool. If I 'appens to be around the farmhouse at tea-time I usually 'elps myself to a few. She makes so many she never misses the odd one or two — dozen that is.

Makes 12—15 scones

Utensils needed: Baking sheet, 2 knives, sieve, measuring spoons, 2-inch (5cm) pastry cutter, large bowl, fork, oven-gloves.

Oven temperature: Gas mark 7, 425°F, 220°C. Before you collect all the ingredients, ask a grown-up to light the oven for you and to make sure there is a shelf near the top of the oven for you to use.

Cooking time: 12–15 minutes.

Ingredients:
   8 ounces (225g) plain flour
   2 level teaspoons baking powder
   1 level teaspoon salt
   1 ounce (25g) butter or block margarine – used
      straight from the fridge
   1 ounce (25g) cooking fat
   ¼ pint (1½dl) milk

Method:
   Sieve the flour, baking powder and salt into the
bowl, then put in the butter or margarine and
cooking fat. Take a knife in each hand and, criss-
crossing them like scissors, cut the fat into the
flour. When the fat is in small pieces put the

Criss-cross the knives to cut up the fat

knives down and use your fingertips to crumble the fat and flour together until it is like bread-crumbs. Using one of the knives, stir in the milk to make a light dough. If the mixture seems too sticky add a little more flour, if too crumbly or dry, add a little more milk. Turn the dough onto a floured surface, put some flour on your hands and knead the dough until it is nice and smooth. Pat out the dough until it is about $\frac{1}{2}$ inch (1cm) thick then, using the pastry cutter, cut out 2 inch (5cm) rounds and place them on the *ungreased* baking sheet. Knead all the odd bits of dough together, pat them out again and cut out some more scones until it is all used up. Prick the tops with the fork.

Put the scones into the oven and bake for 12–15 minutes, or until they are well risen and golden on top. Eat while they are still warm with butter and jam.

BUTTERSCOTCH RAISIN DELIGHT

This 'ere recipe's so easy even you titchy yumans could make it without mucking it up.

Serves 4 people

Utensils needed: 1 small bowl, 1 medium-sized bowl, 2 jugs, 1 tablespoon, 1 teaspoon, sieve, whisk, 4 small dishes.

Ingredients:
    2 tablespoons raisins
    ¼ pint (1½dl) hot water
    1 packet Butterscotch Angel Delight
    ½ pint (3dl) cold milk
    1 teaspoon instant coffee essence

Method:

Place the raisins in the small bowl, carefully pour on the hot water and leave them to soak for an hour or two, until they are nice and plump. Strain them into a sieve and throw away the water. Make up the Angel Delight with the cold milk as directed on the packet, stirring in the coffee essence and the raisins. Spoon into the small dishes and chill them in the fridge for half an hour before serving.